GEOGRAPHY FOR KIDS

PATTERNS, LOCATION AND INTERRELATIONSHIPS

THE WORLD IN SPATIAL TERMS

3rd Grade Social Studies

Speedy Publishing LLC

40 E. Main St. #1156

Newark, DE 19711

www.speedypublishing.com

Copyright 2017

In this book, we're going to talk all about geography. So, let's get right to it!

WHAT IS GEOGRAPHY?

Geography is the study of the physical features of planet Earth. It's also the study of how human beings influence the environment and how it influences them. There are three important questions that relate to the study of geography:

- How do people use Earth's resources?

- How do people interact with their environment, including living and nonliving things?

How does the Earth's land, air, water, and soil influence the way people live?

PHYSICAL GEOGRAPHY VERSUS CULTURAL GEOGRAPHY

When geographers research a location, they may take a small region, such as a town, or they may research an entire country. Sometimes their studies focus on the whole world.

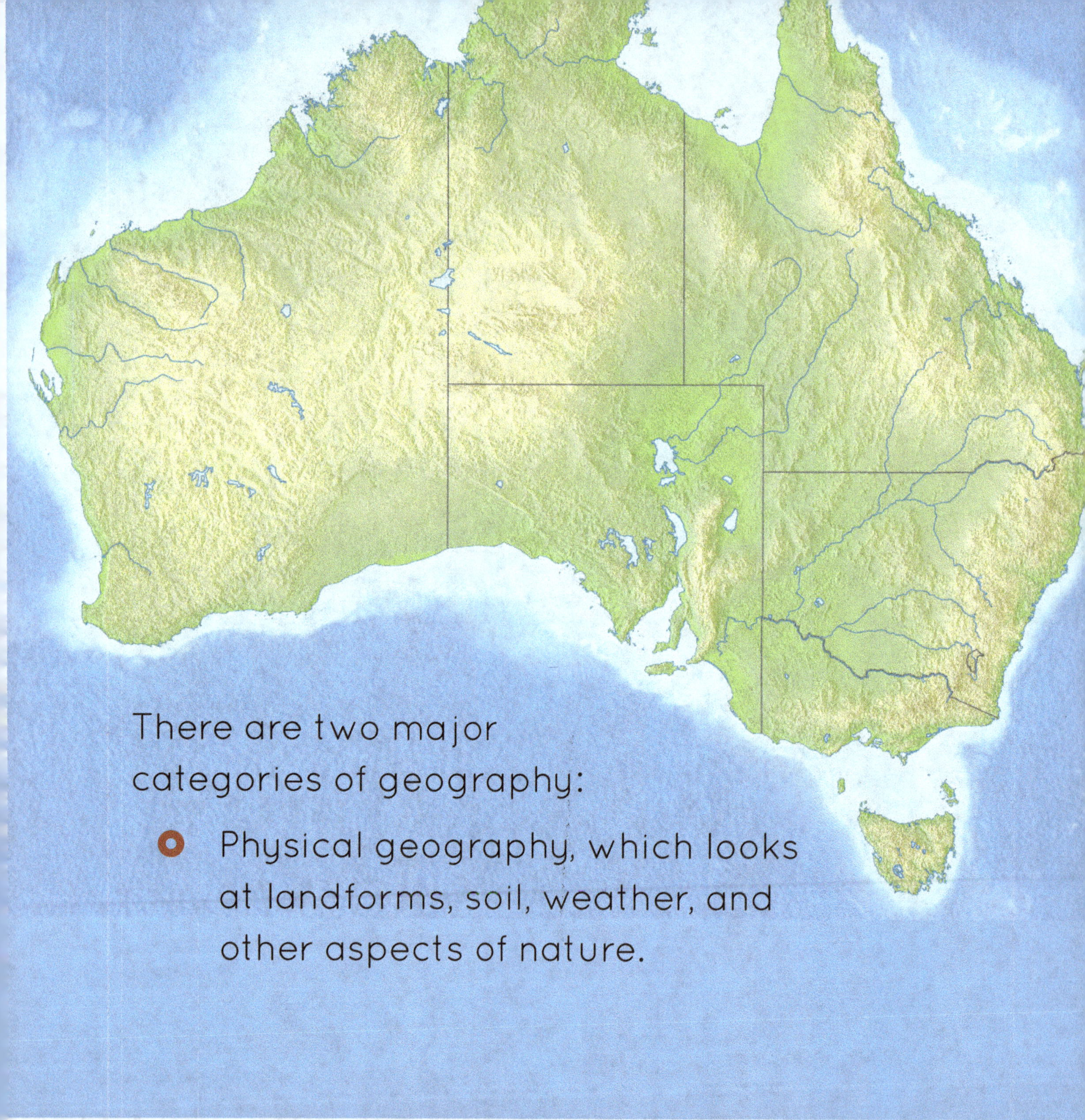

There are two major
categories of geography:

- Physical geography, which looks
  at landforms, soil, weather, and
  other aspects of nature.

FOLK ART OF SWITZERLAND

- Cultural geography, which looks at how human beings interact with each other as well as their environment.

When people inhabit an area, they use the area's natural resources. They shape their environment by farming and building. They also use the cultural resources by working together to pool their creativity, practical skills, and knowledge.

COLORED SAND ART,
ORIGINATING IN CEARÁ

GEOGRAPHY TOOLS

Geographers use maps and globes to help them define areas they want to study. Both of these types of tools are very useful, but they have disadvantages as well. A globe is a spherical model of the Earth. Because it's shaped like the Earth is actually shaped in reality, it shows the major landmasses and waterways accurately in relationship to each other.

0
30
60
90

N

NE

E

SE

S

APAN

Lhasa

ARU

Gyan

BHUTAN   Bomdila

IMPHU   Tezpu

ASSAM Naga

Guwahati DISPUR

SHILONG

MEGHALAYA

Sylhet

pur BANGLADESH

pur AGARTALA

ol DHAKA   TRIPURA

WEST BENGAL

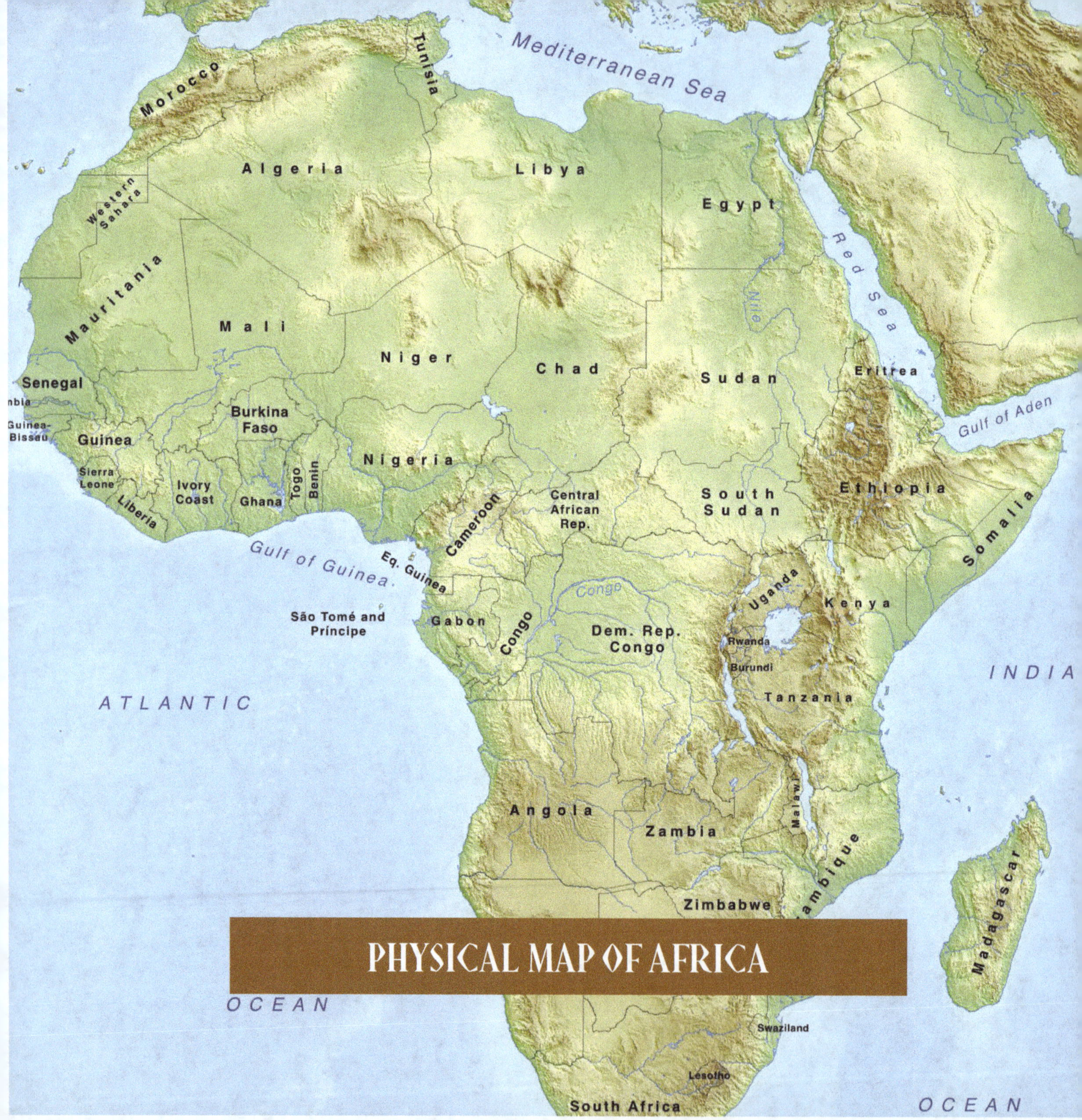

Mediterranean Sea
Morocco
Tunisia
Algeria
Libya
Egypt
Western Sahara
Mauritania
Mali
Niger
Chad
Sudan
Red Sea
Nile
Eritrea
Senegal
Gambia
Guinea-Bissau
Guinea
Burkina Faso
Sierra Leone
Liberia
Ivory Coast
Ghana
Togo
Benin
Nigeria
Central African Rep.
South Sudan
Ethiopia
Gulf of Aden
Somalia
Cameroon
Eq. Guinea
Gulf of Guinea
São Tomé and Príncipe
Gabon
Congo
Congo
Dem. Rep. Congo
Uganda
Rwanda
Burundi
Kenya
Tanzania
ATLANTIC
INDIA
Angola
Zambia
Malawi
Mozambique
Zimbabwe
Madagascar
Swaziland
Lesotho
South Africa
OCEAN
OCEAN
PHYSICAL MAP OF AFRICA

n the other hand, maps take a portion of the Earth's surface, which is curved, and represent it as a flat drawing. Because of this, no flat map can show landmasses or waterways in accurate detail. In fact, the larger the region of the world a map depicts, the more inaccurate its relative sizes will be. If you compare the way the country of Greenland and the continent of Australia look on both a globe and a map, you'll see the type of distortion that occurs on a map.

Despite this problem, maps are still very useful since they can show small regions with lots of details. There's no way that you could carry around a globe that would show all the details of cities or highways!

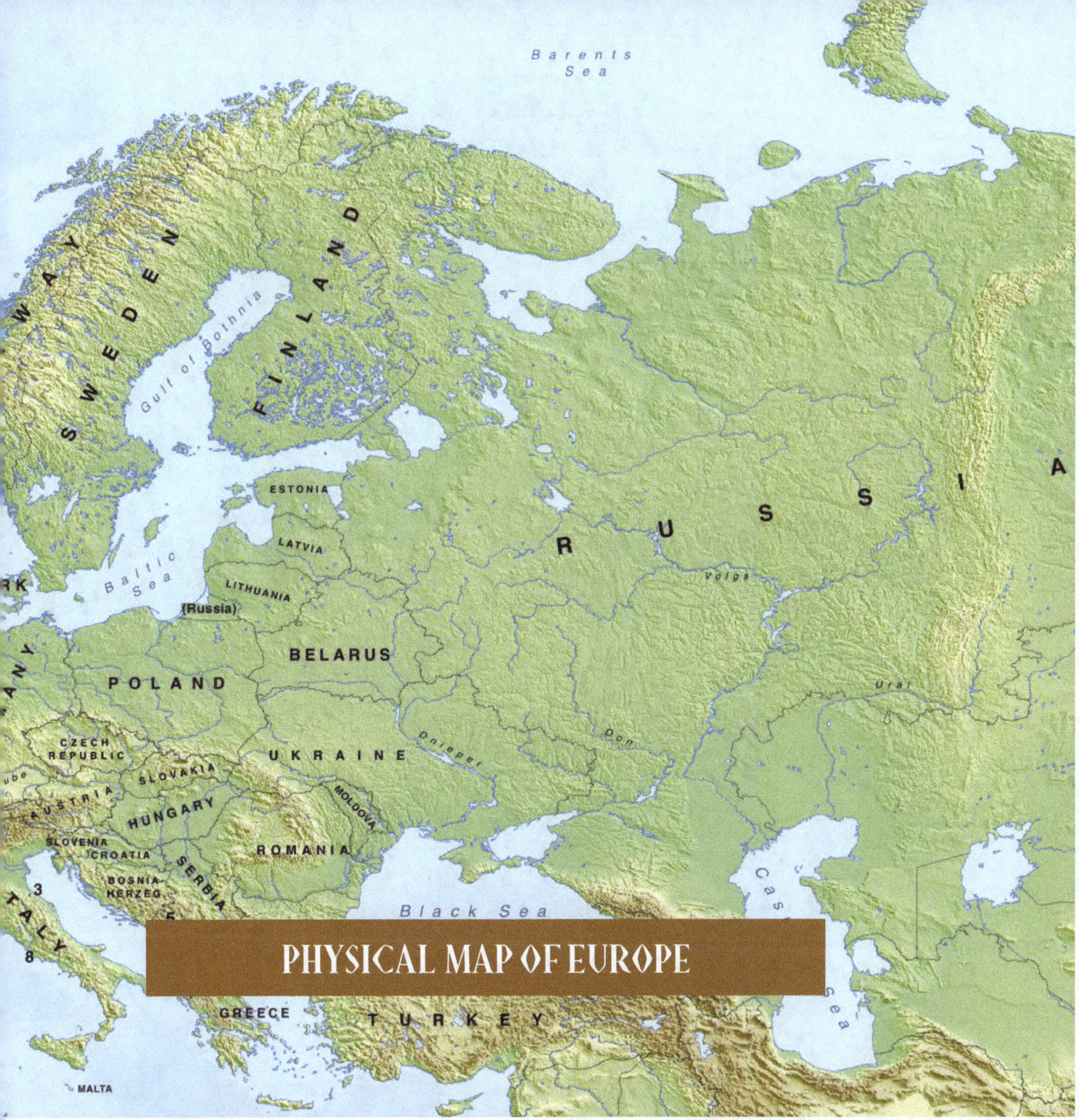

PHYSICAL MAP OF EUROPE

LATITUDE AND LONGITUDE

In order to divide physical maps into areas for study, geographers created a system that works like a grid. They use a system of imaginary lines to identify specific locations on Earth. A map is divided by these horizontal and vertical lines. Using these lines, which are called latitude and longitude, in tandem with the directions of north and south as well as east and west, you can pinpoint locations on Earth.

The top of the Earth is the North Pole and the South Pole is located at its bottom. The equator runs around the center of the Earth at its widest diameter.

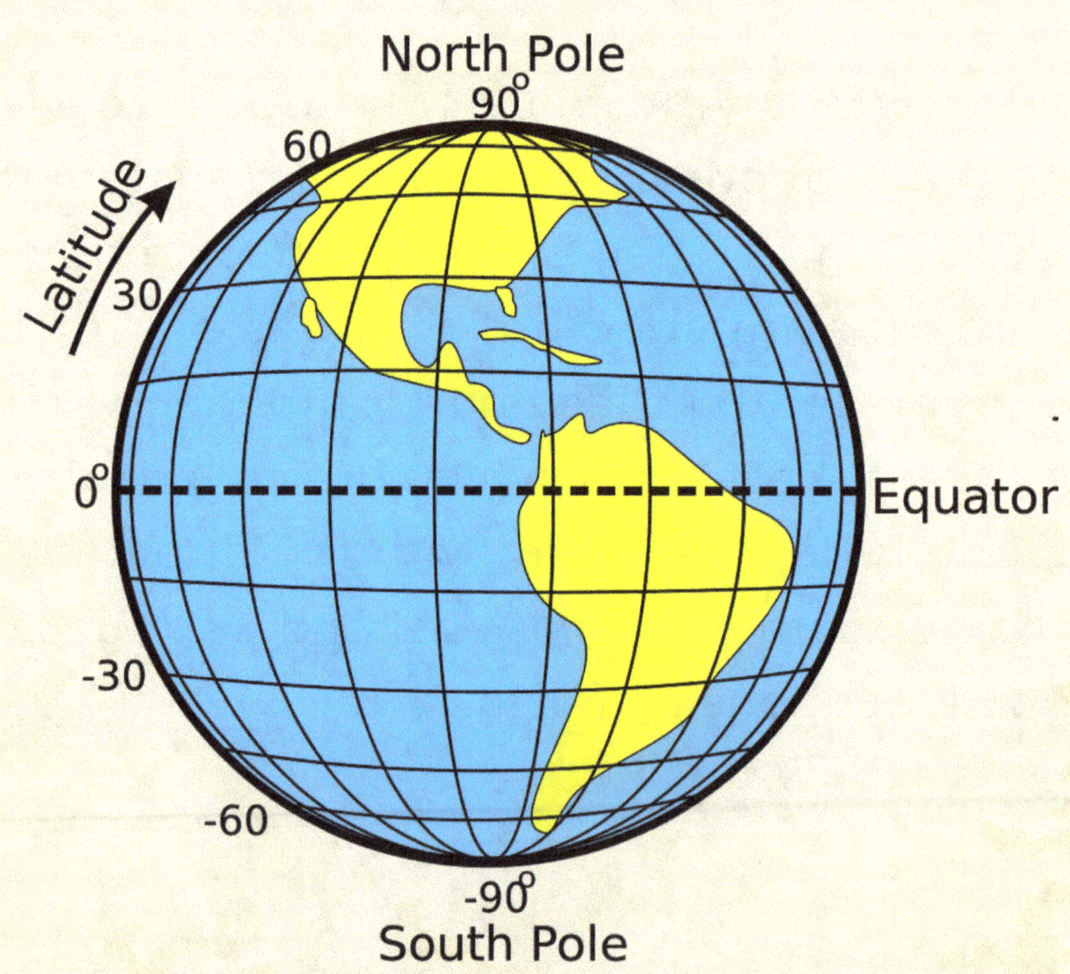

It is halfway between the North and South Poles. Everything north of the equator is in the Northern half or hemisphere of the Earth and everything south of the equator is in the Southern half or hemisphere of the Earth.

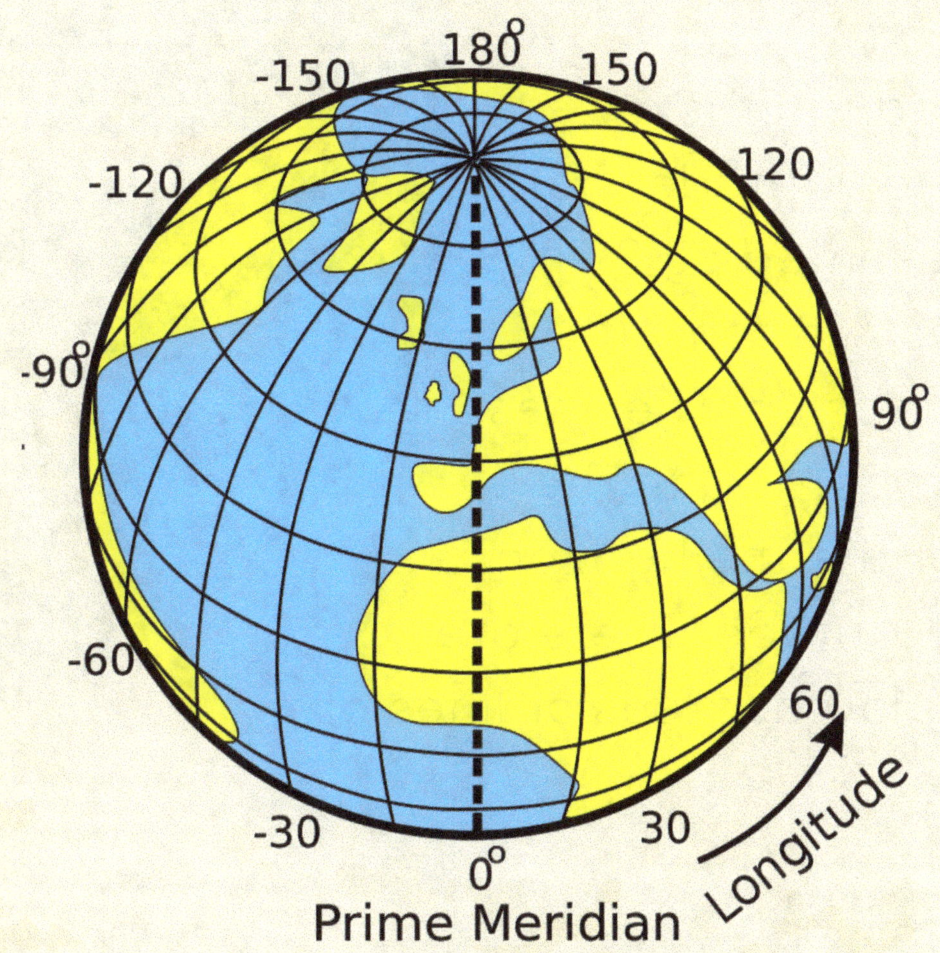

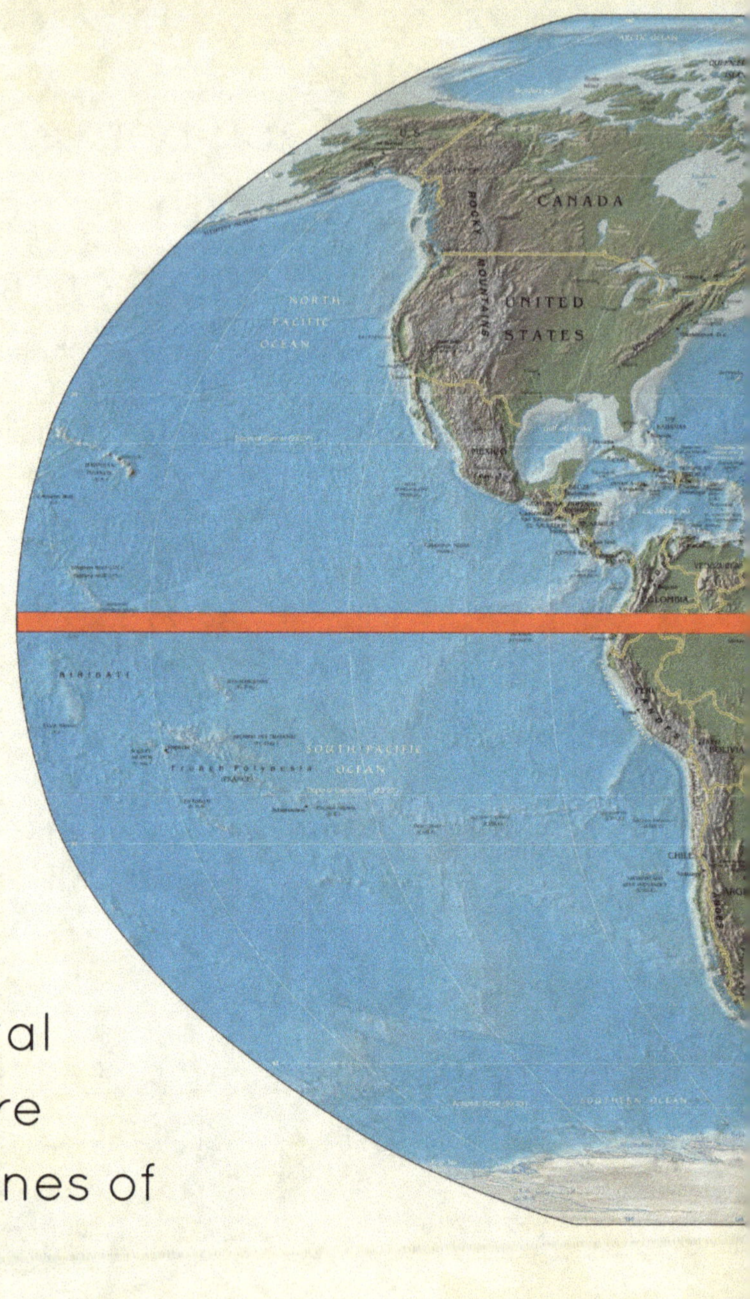

The equator is a line of latitude that is represented by 0 degrees, written with symbols as 0°. The lines running parallel to the equator are the horizontal lines of latitude. There are exactly 180 degrees or lines of latitude.

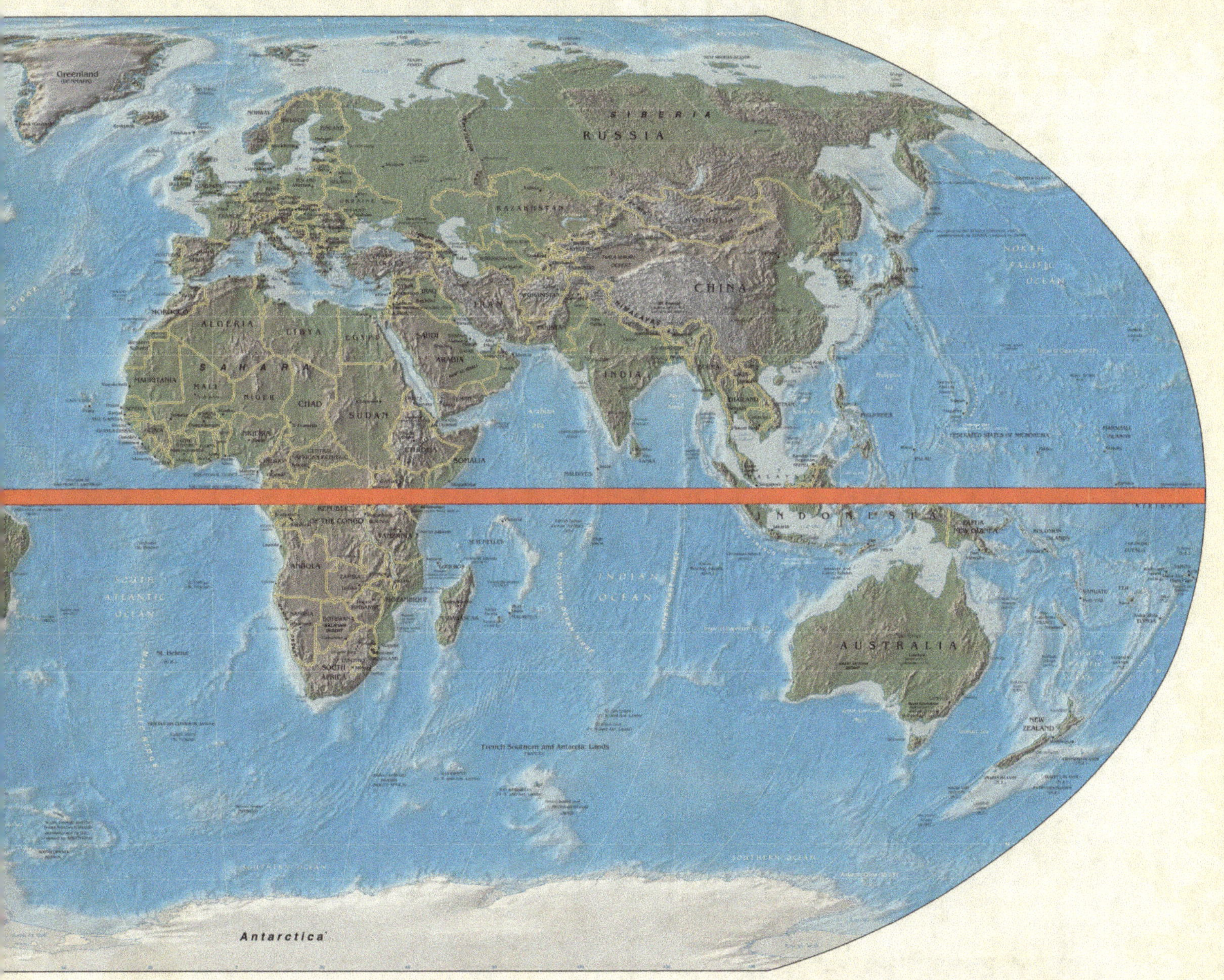

WORLD MAP WITH EQUATOR

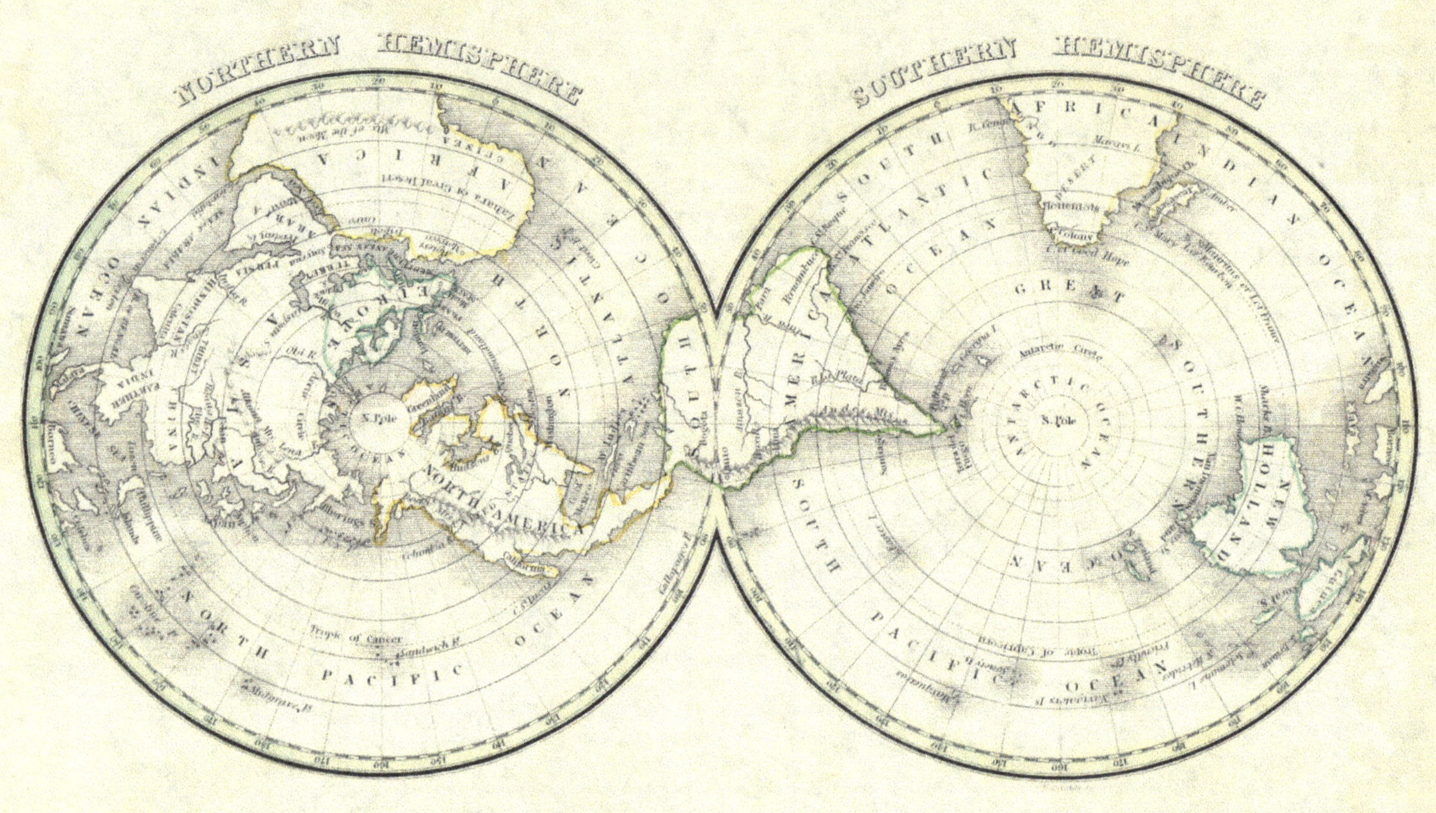

1838 BRADFORD MAP OF THE WORLD ON POLAR PROJECTION

The equator was an easy way to separate the Earth into a Northern and Southern Hemisphere, but to describe an Eastern and Western Hemisphere geographers needed to pick a starting point. They selected the location of Greenwich in the country of England. The line of longitude that travels through Greenwich is described as the Prime Meridian of 0 degrees of longitude.

Along with the Prime Meridian, the line of longitude on Earth's opposite side at the 180-degree position, divides the Earth into Eastern and Western Hemispheres.

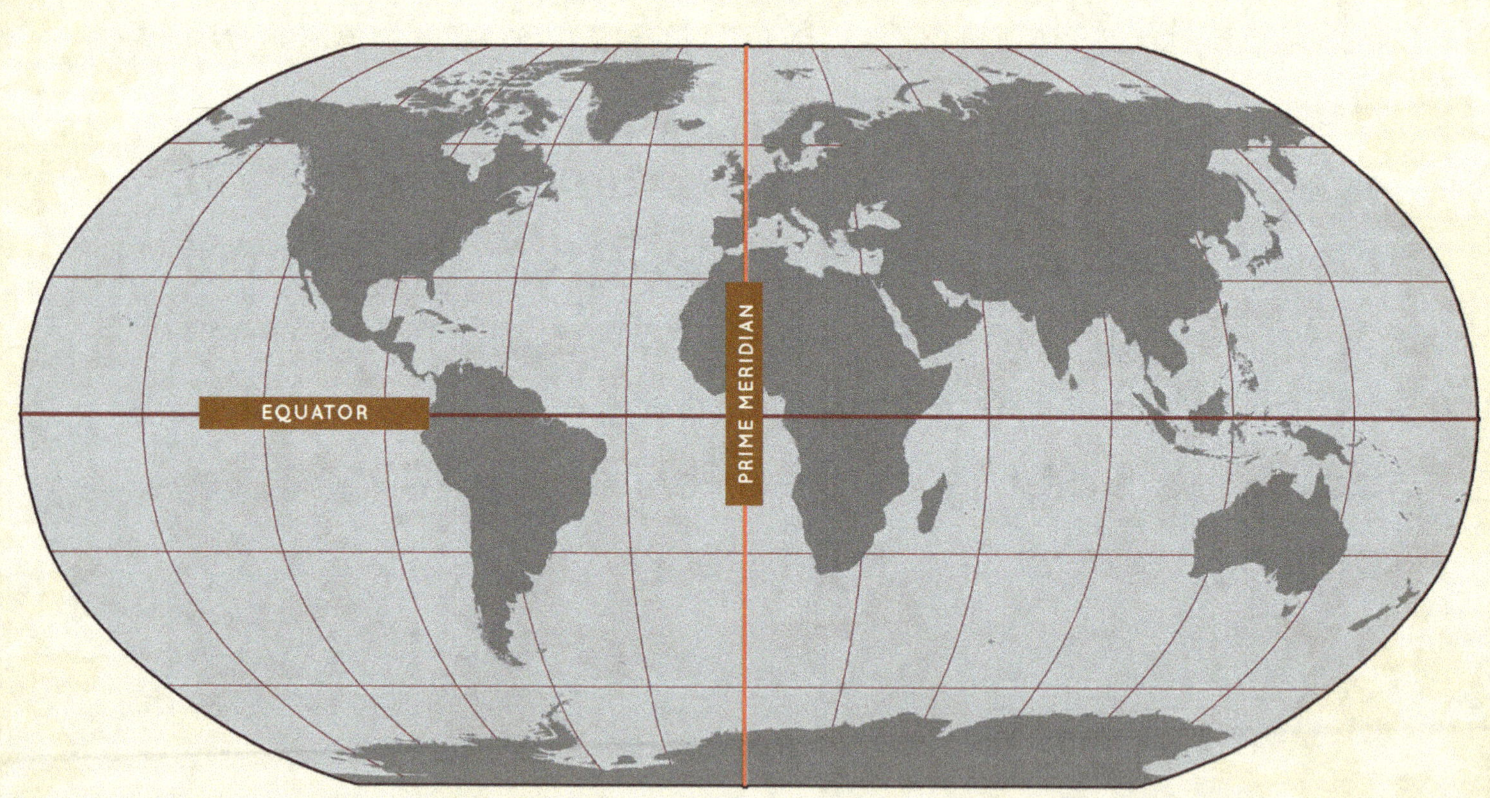

There are 360 lines or degrees of longitude. Longitude specifies time zones, but both latitude and longitude are necessary to pinpoint locations.

CLIMATE AND HEMISPHERES

The seasonal tilt of Earth, either toward the Sun or away from it, gives us the change in seasons. In the Northern Hemisphere, the summer months are from the month of June through the month of September. When people in the Northern Hemisphere are experiencing winter, those in the Southern Hemisphere are experiencing summer, beginning in December and ending in March.

EARTH'S NORTHERN HEMISPHERE
WITH SEA ICE AND CLOUDS

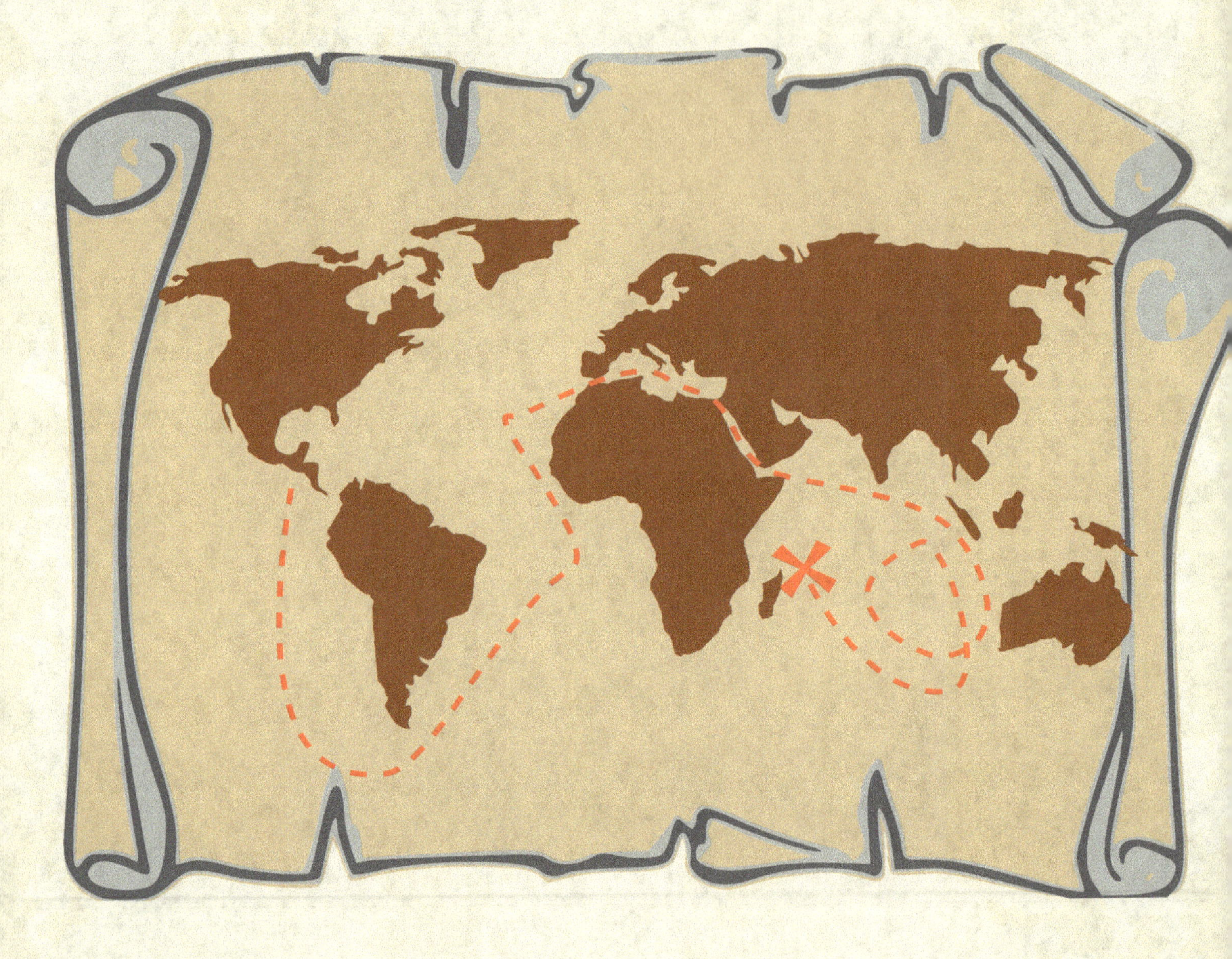

TYPES OF MAPS

There are many different types of maps that geographers, other scientists, and scholars use. Maps are available in both print and digital form. Digital maps are available on mobile devices. Here are some of the more common types of maps:

These types of maps show the physical characteristics of a place such as mountains and lakes.

Waterways are depicted using blue. The color green is used for elevations that are lower, and brown is used for higher elevations.

TOPOGRAPHICAL MAP

These types of maps also depict physical features. However, instead of using colors for elevations, curved lines are used. These lines, which are called contour lines, show the changes in elevation by 100-foot increments. When the lines are close together, it means the terrain is very steep. When they are far apart, it means the terrain is somewhat flat.

A
Topographical Map
OF THE
WHITE MOUNTAINS,
OF
NEW HAMPSHIRE.
By C.H. Hitchcock.
OSGOOD'S
WHITE MOUNTAIN
GUIDE BOOK
CONNECTICUT RIVER
Lancaster
Whitefield
Littleton
Bethlehem
Woodstock
Thornton
Campton Village
West Campton
SCALE. 3 MILES TO AN INCH: (⅓ size of model)
71°50'   71°40'   71°30'   71°20'   71°10'
44°30'   44°20'   44°10'

CAPE VERDE
Praia
MOROCCO
Rabat
WESTERN SAHARA
ALGERIA
TUNISIA
Tunis
Valetta
Tripoli
LIBYA
Athens
Nicosia
Beirut
Damascus
Jerusalem
Amman
Cairo
Baghdad
Kuwait
Teheran
Manama
Doha
Riyadh
EGYPT
MAURITANIA
Nouakchott
MALI
NIGER
CHAD
SUDAN
ERITREA
Asamara
Sanaa
Dakar
SENEGAL
Niamey
Ndjamena
DJIBOUTI
SOMALILAND (disputed)
Hargeysa
Banjul
GAMBIA
Ouagadougou
BURKINA FASO
NIGERIA
Bissau
GUINEA-BISSAU
GUINEA
Conakry
SIERRA LEONE
Freetown
CÔTE D'IVOIRE
GHANA
TOGO
BENIN
Abuja
Addis Ababa
ETHIOPIA
SOMALIA
LIBERIA
Monrovia
Yamoussoukro
Accra
Lome
Cotonou
CAMEROON
CENTRAL AFRICAN REPUBLIC
SOUTH SUDAN
Abidjan
Malabo
Yaounde
Bangui
Mogadishu
EQUATORIAL GUINEA
Sao Tome
SAO TOMÉ AND PRÍNCIPE
Libreville
GABON
CONGO
UGANDA
KENYA
DR CONGO
RWANDA
Kigali
Kampala
Nairobi
Brazzaville
BURUNDI
Kinshasa
Bujumbura
COMOROS
Moroni
Luanda
TANZANIA
Dar es Salaam
ANGOLA
ZAMBIA
MALAWI
Lilongwe
Lusaka
MOZAMBIQUE
Harare
ZIMBABWE
MADAGASCAR
Antananarivo
NAMIBIA
BOTSWANA
Windhoek
Gaborone
Pretoria
Maputo
Mbabane
SWAZILAND
Bloemfontein
Maseru
LESOTHO
SOUTH AFRICA

POLITICAL MAP

A political map shows the boundaries of states and nations. For example, a map of the United States showing the state borders, as well as the borders with the countries of Canada and Mexico, would be a political map.

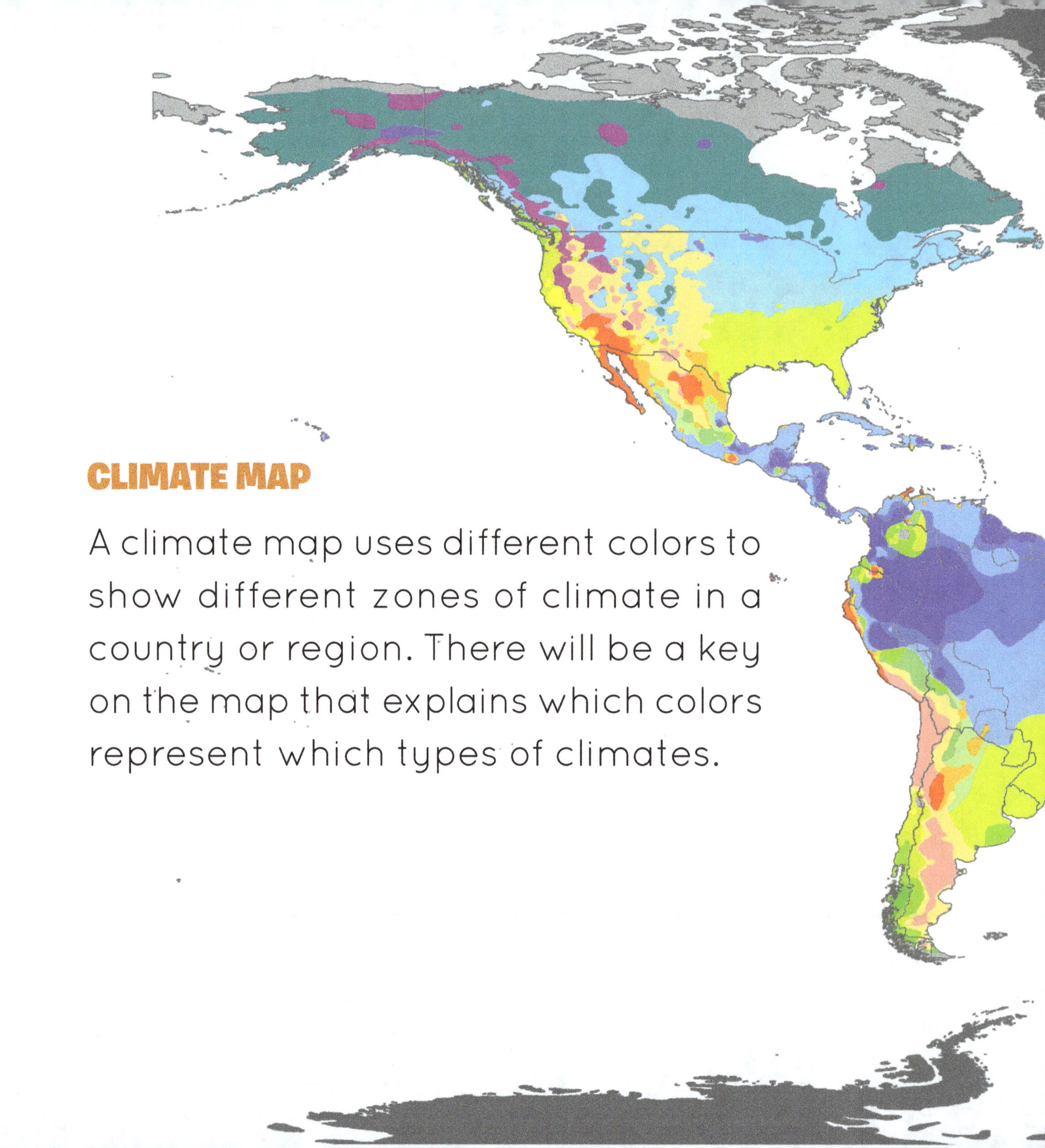

CLIMATE MAP

A climate map uses different colors to show different zones of climate in a country or region. There will be a key on the map that explains which colors represent which types of climates.

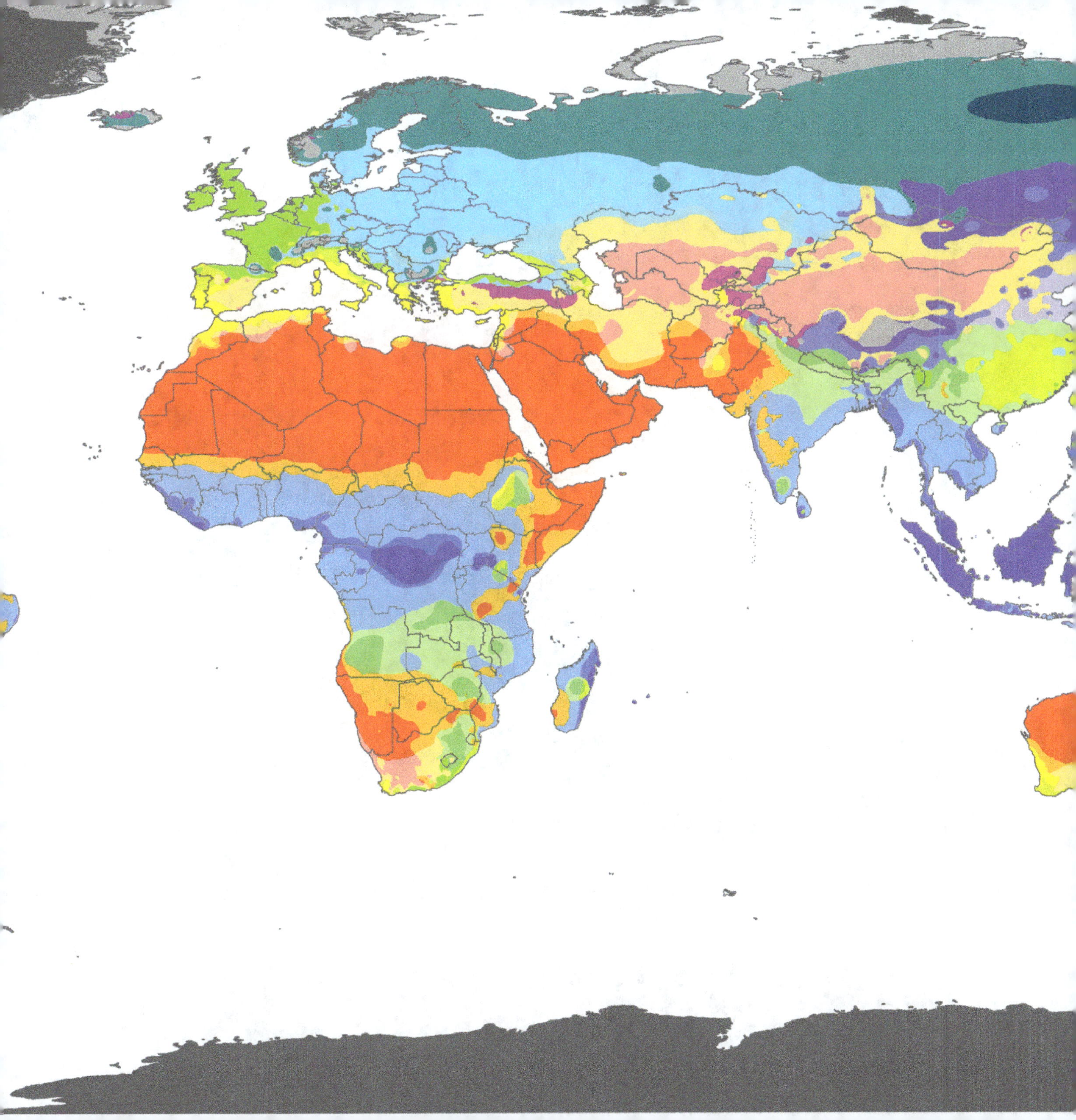

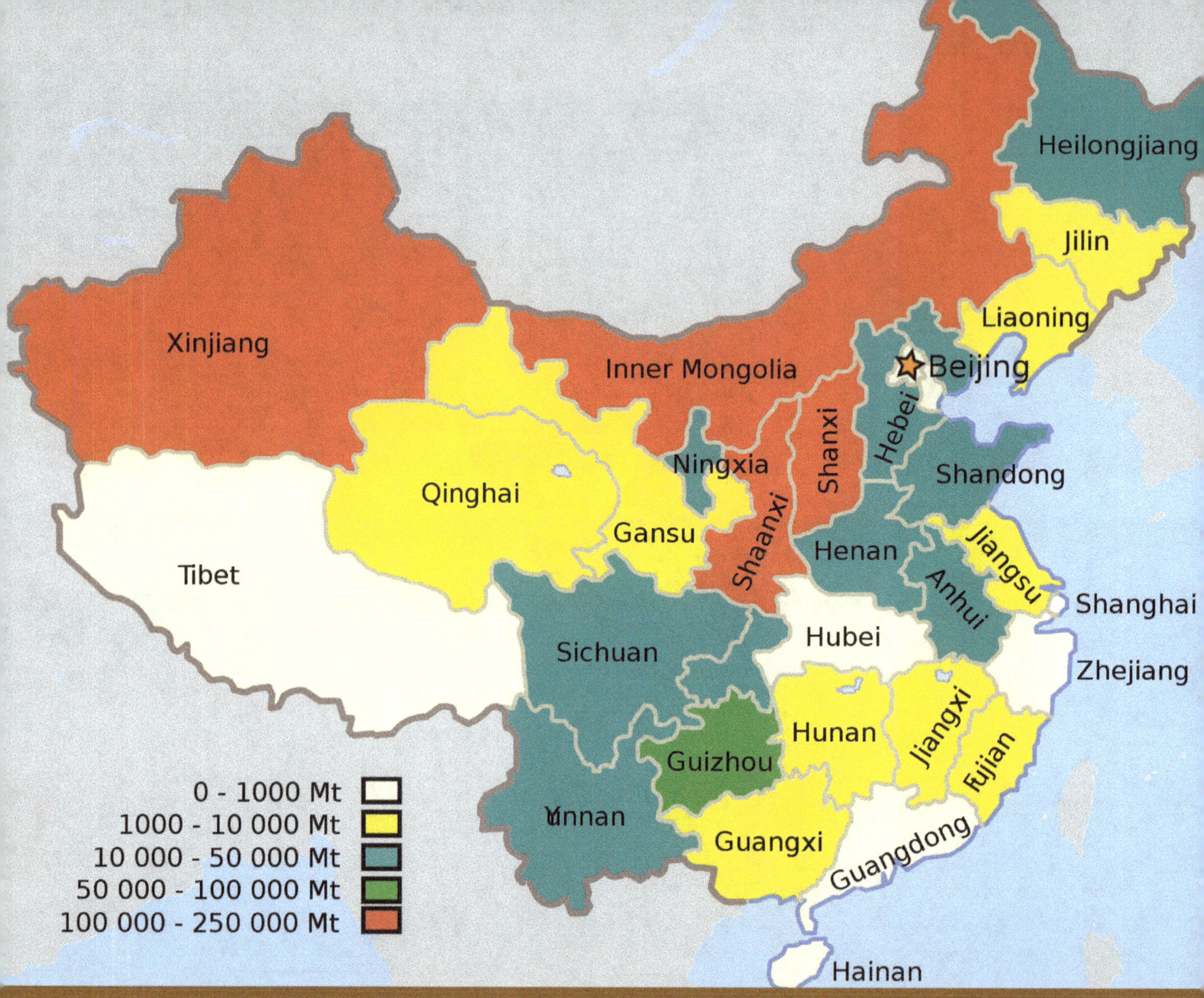

MAP OF CHINA COAL RESOURCES

ECONOMIC OR RESOURCE MAP

This type of map uses different symbols to represent agricultural products, natural resources, or energy sources. Once again, there will be a key or legend on the map that tells what the different symbols signify.

ROAD MAP

This is the type of map that many everyday people use to get from place to place. It shows highways, roads, airports, locations of cities, and places of interest. Interstate highways are depicted with wider lines than the state highways.

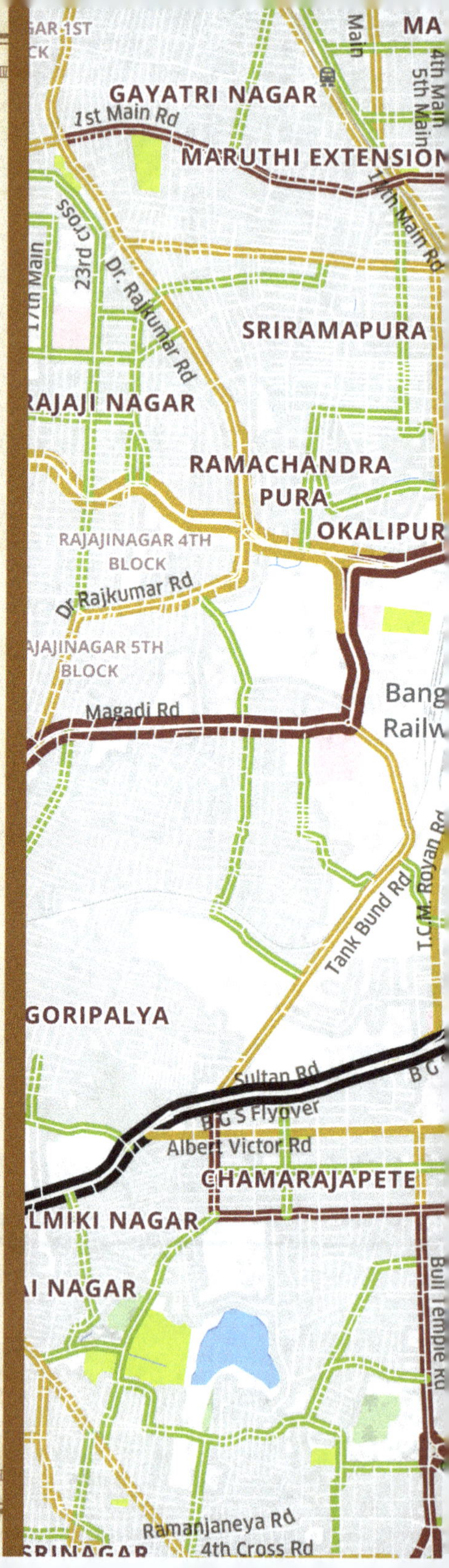

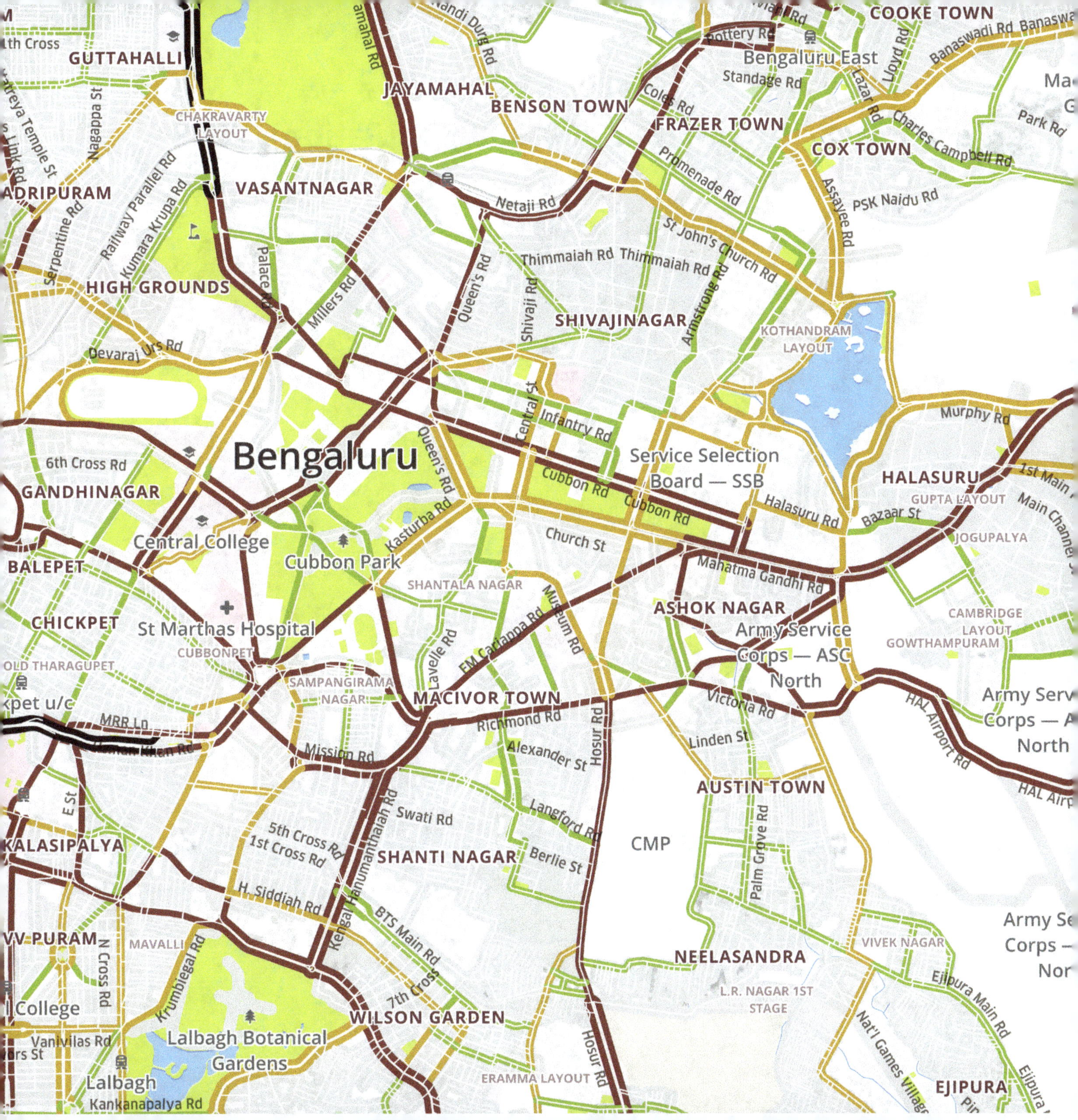

GUTTAHALLI
JAYAMAHAL
BENSON TOWN
COOKE TOWN
Bengaluru East
FRAZER TOWN
COX TOWN
VASANTNAGAR
Netaji Rd
Promenade Rd
Coles Rd
Standage Rd
Charles Campbell Rd
Park Rd
ADRIPURAM
CHAKRAVARTY LAYOUT
St John's Church Rd
PSK Naidu Rd
Assayee Rd
HIGH GROUNDS
Millers Rd
Queen's Rd
Shivaji Rd
Thimmaiah Rd
Thimmaiah Rd
SHIVAJINAGAR
Armstrong Rd
KOTHANDRAM LAYOUT
Devaraj Urs Rd
Central St
Infantry Rd
Murphy Rd
Bengaluru
Queen's Rd
Service Selection Board — SSB
HALASURU
1st Main
GUPTA LAYOUT
Main Channel
6th Cross Rd
Cubbon Rd
Cubbon Rd
Halasuru Rd
Bazaar St
JOGUPALYA
GANDHINAGAR
Kasturba Rd
Church St
Central College
Cubbon Park
Mahatma Gandhi Rd
BALEPET
SHANTALA NAGAR
CAMBRIDGE LAYOUT
GOWTHAMPURAM
CHICKPET
St Marthas Hospital
ASHOK NAGAR
Army Service Corps — ASC North
CUBBONPET
Lavelle Rd
Museum Rd
FM Cariappa Rd
OLD THARAGUPET
SAMPANGIRAMA NAGAR
Army Serv Corps — A North
kpet u/c
MACIVOR TOWN
Victoria Rd
HAL Airport Rd
MRR Ln
Richmond Rd
Hosur Rd
Linden St
Mission Rd
Alexander St
HAL Airp
E St
Langford Rd
AUSTIN TOWN
Swati Rd
Berlie St
Palm Grove Rd
KALASIPALYA
5th Cross Rd
1st Cross Rd
SHANTI NAGAR
CMP
Kengal Hanumanthaiah Rd
H. Siddiah Rd
VV PURAM
MAVALLI
BTS Main Rd
VIVEK NAGAR
Army Se Corps — Nor
NEELASANDRA
College
Krumbiegal Rd
7th Cross
L.R. NAGAR 1ST STAGE
Ejipura Main Rd
Vanivilas Rd
WILSON GARDEN
Hosur Rd
Nat'l Games Village
Lalbagh Botanical Gardens
Lalbagh
Kankanapalya Rd
ERAMMA LAYOUT
EJIPURA

Injury mortality rate (per 100,000 population), 2008

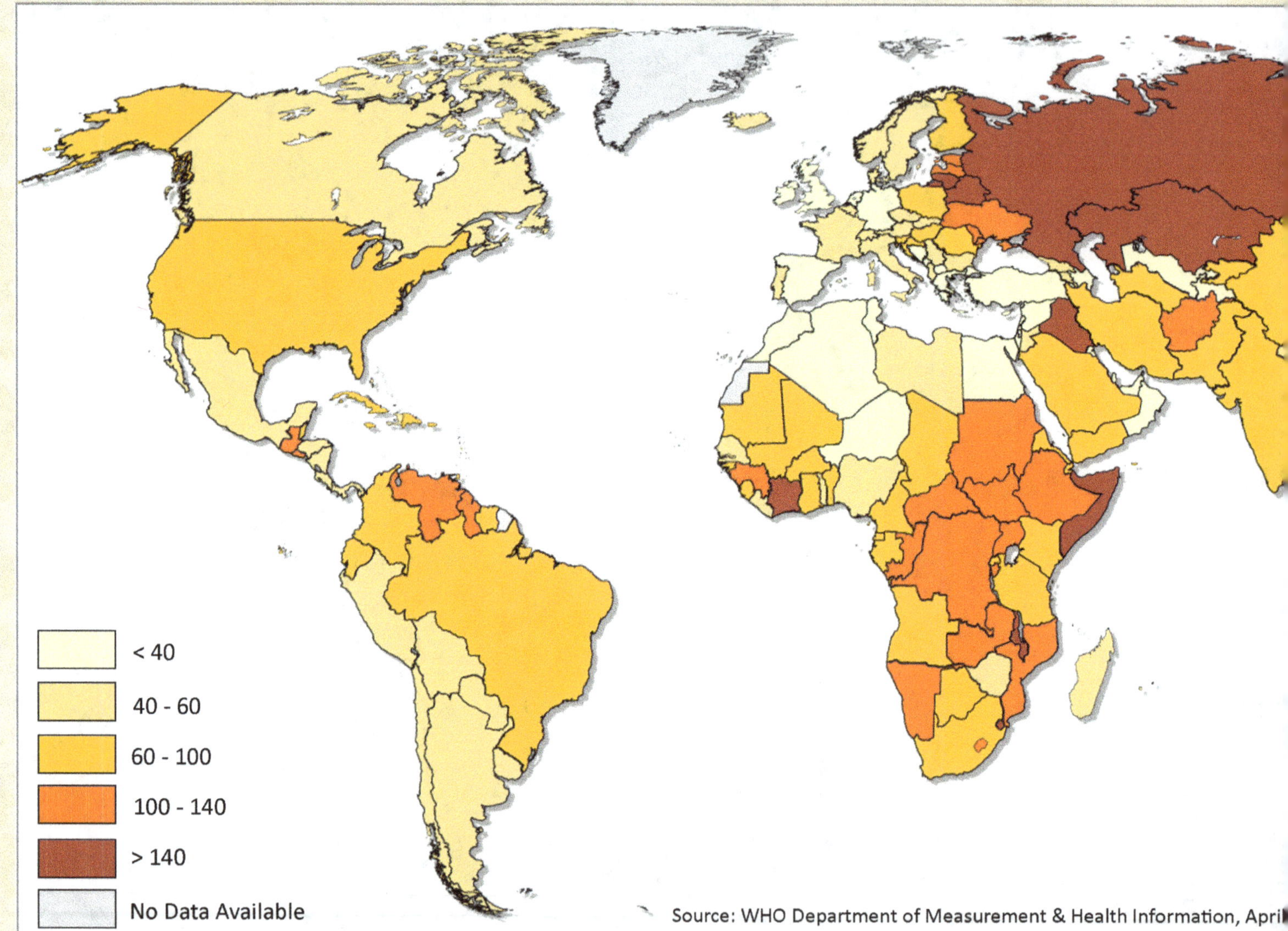

THEMATIC MAP

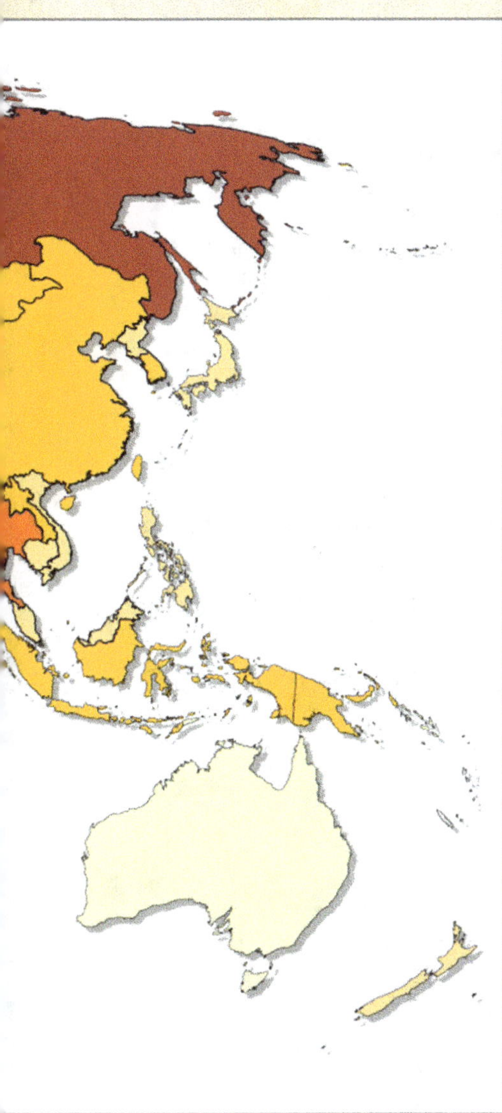

Thematic maps are becoming more popular and more common. They are based on a specific set of data. For example, a map could show the spread of a disease throughout a region, or the average snowfall for a specific location, or the change in population over time in a designated area. As more and more data is becoming collected, there will be new types of maps to give quick visual snapshots of the information in a way that is easy to use.

GEOGRAPHIC REGIONS

Geographers frequently talk about geographic regions. Regions are specified by a certain physical or cultural characteristic. For example, the Amazon Basin, which is located in South America, is a physical region associated with the Amazon River and its tributaries.

Atlantic Ocean
Pacific Ocean
VENEZUELA
Caracas
Bogotá
COLOMBIA
GUYANA
Georgetown
Quito
ECUADOR
PERU
Lima
Iquitos
BOLIVIA
La Paz
Cochabamba
Santa Cruz
BRAZIL
Brasília
Belém
Macapá
Manaus
Sanatarém
Imperatr
Rio Branco
Porto Velho
Pucallpa
Cusco
São Paulo
Rio d Jane
Vaupés
Apaporis
Caquetá
Napo
Tigre
astafa
Marañón
Huallaga
Ucayali
Javary
Tambo
Mantaro
Ene
Apurimac
Juruá
Purus
Putumayo
Japurá
Negro
Branco
Trombetas
Paru
Jari
Para
Madeira
Machado
Guaporé
Beni
Mamoré
Grande
Acre
Madre de Dios
Tapajós
Juruena
Arinos
Teles Pires
Xingu
Iriri
Araguaia
Tocantins

The Gobi Desert would be another region that is associated with a physical characteristic. The New York metropolitan region is a cultural region because it is associated with the population and culture of New York.

READING MAPS

The title of a map will give you clues as to what the mapmaker intended to depict on the map. Good quality maps have legends that explain the different symbols that are used on the map. For example, a square that has a flag positioned on the top of it generally represents a school.

1:125000
MÜNC

Different types of roads are depicted with lines of various thicknesses and colors. Dashed lines sometimes represent borders.

However, symbols on maps published in the United States may represent something different in other countries.

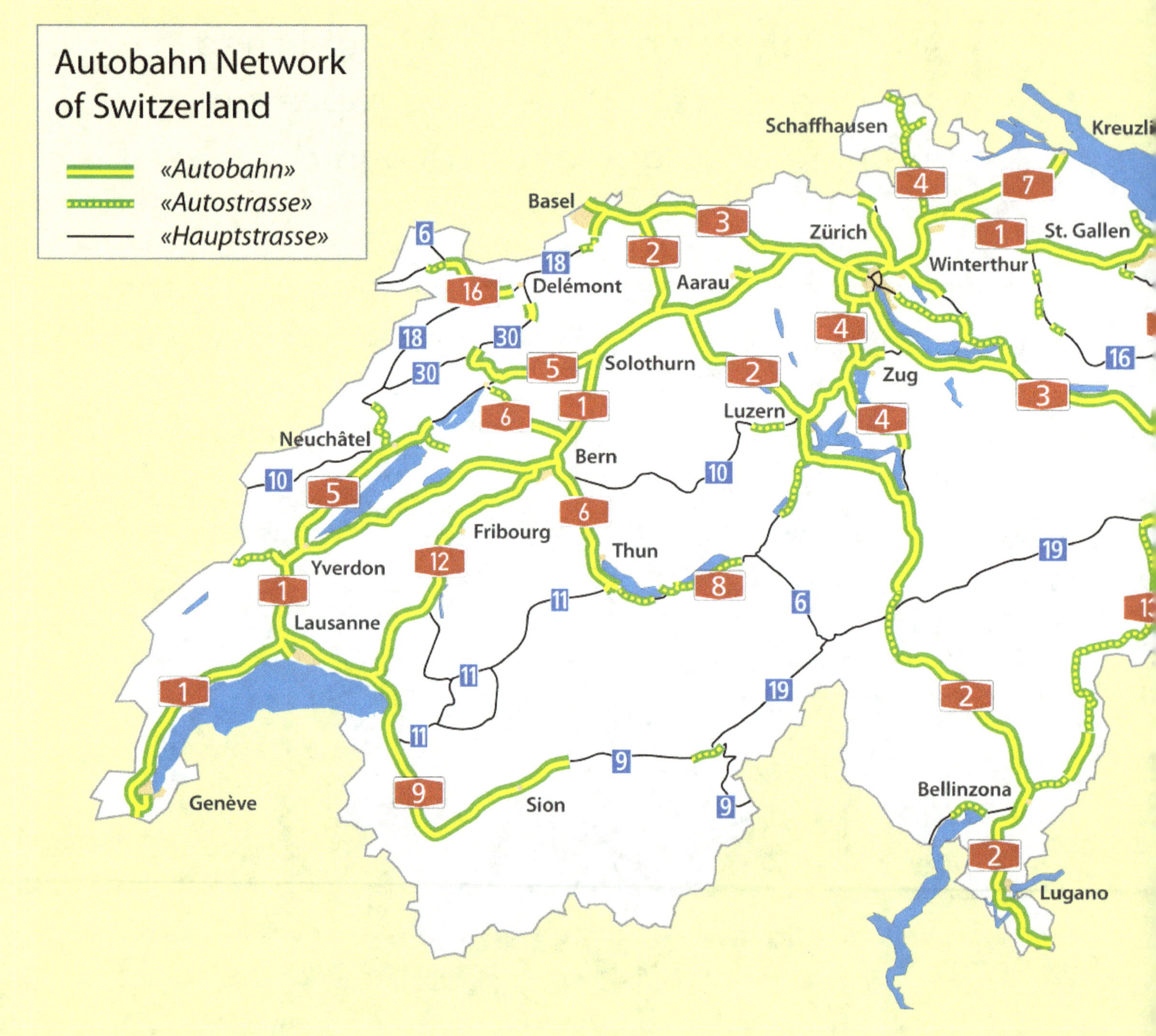

Autobahn Network
of Switzerland
«Autobahn»
«Autostrasse»
«Hauptstrasse»
Schaffhausen
Kreuzli
Basel
Zürich
Winterthur
St. Gallen
Delémont
Aarau
Solothurn
Zug
Luzern
Neuchâtel
Bern
Fribourg
Thun
Yverdon
Lausanne
Genève
Sion
Bellinzona
Lugano

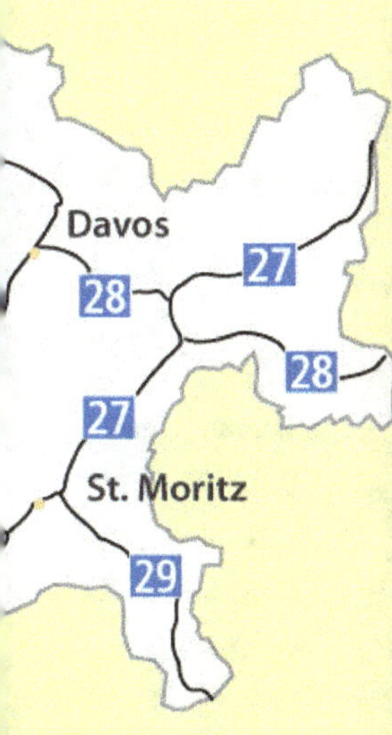

For example, on a Swiss map the symbol used for a railroad is the same symbol used on some topographical maps for secondary highways in the United States. Make sure you study the key or legend so you know what the symbols mean.

A map should have an arrow that designates which way is north. Some topographic maps point to the North Pole as true north and also to where your compass directs, which is magnetic north in the northern regions of Canada.

Washington
Oregon
Idaho
Montana
North Dakota
Minnesota
Wisconsin
South Dakota
Wyoming
Nebraska
Iowa
Michigan
New York
New Hampshire
Vermont
Massachusetts
Maine
Nevada
Utah
Colorado
Kansas
Missouri
Illinois
Indiana
Ohio
Pennsylvania
Rhode Island
Connecticut
New Jersey
Delaware
California
Arizona
New Mexico
Oklahoma
Arkansas
Tennessee
Kentucky
Virginia
Maryland
Washington, D.C.
West Virginia
North Carolina
Texas
Louisiana
Mississippi
Alabama
Georgia
South Carolina
Florida
Alaska
Hawaii
100 mi
100 km
100 200 300 mi
100 200 300 km
200
200

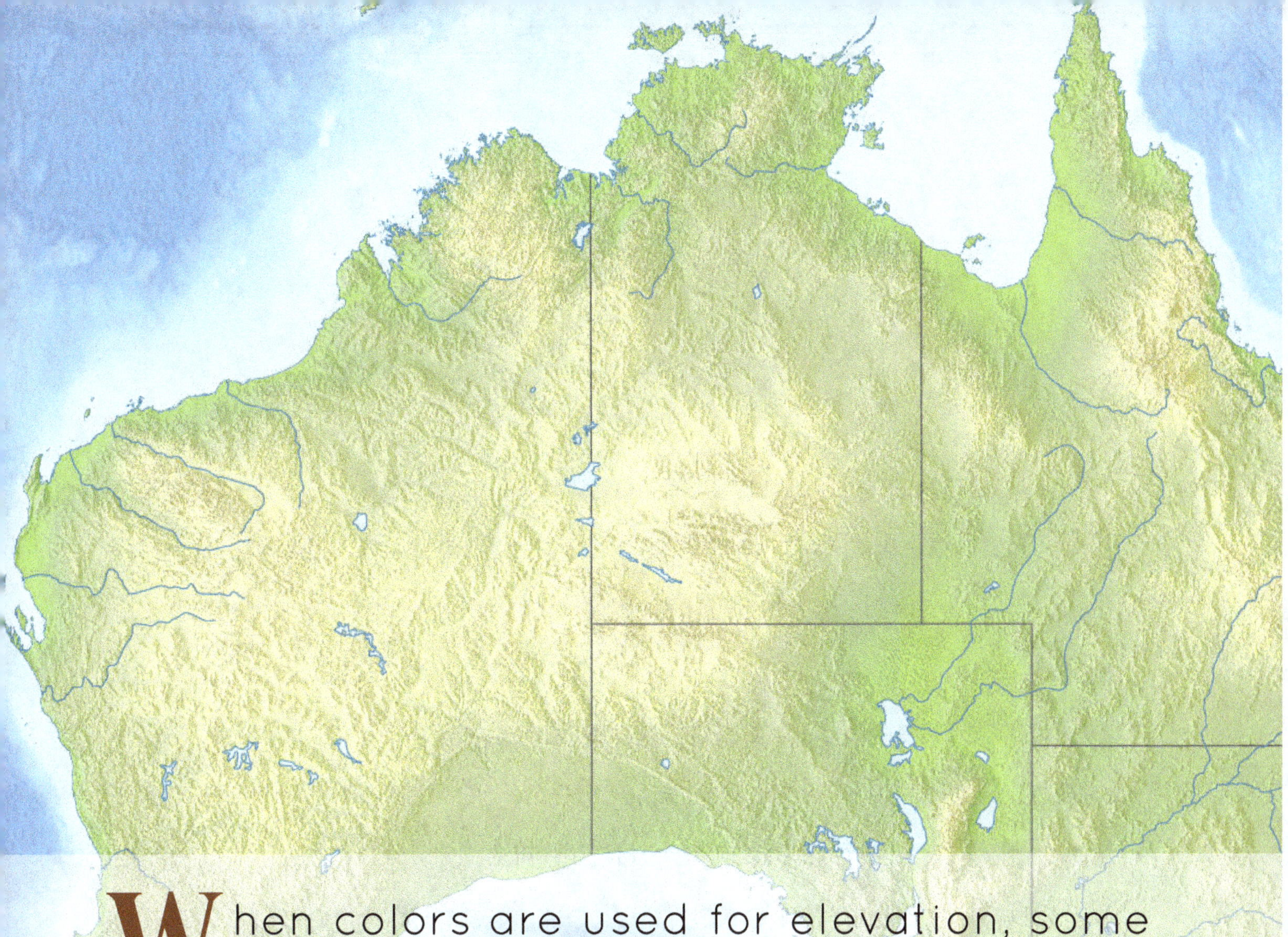

When colors are used for elevation, some people misinterpret it. For example, green is used for lower elevations on physical maps, but we associate green with a fertile farm area when it might be a low-lying desert.

SUMMARY

Geography is the study of the physical features of the Earth. It's also the study of how people use the Earth's resources and interact with all the elements in their environment including other people, plants and animals, and non-living natural resources like soil and water. Geographers make frequent use of globes and different types of maps as they research and make recommendations.

GULF OF MEXICO
INDIANA
Ohio
KENTUCKY
Frankfort
Columbus
OHIO
Nashville
TENN.
Memphis
Chattanooga
Birmingham
Knoxville
Greenville
Charlotte
NORTH CAROLINA
Raleigh
VIRGINIA
Richmond
Wash. D.C.
Charleston
W. VA.
Detroit
Cleve.
ERIE
Toledo
Columbia
SOUTH CAROLINA
Charleston
Savannah
ALABAMA
Montgomery
GEORGIA
Atlanta
Tallahassee
FLORIDA
Jacksonville
Daytona Beach
C. Canaveral
Mobile
Pensacola
New Orleans
LOUISIANA
Jackson
MISS.
Baton Rouge
Tampa
Sarasota
Everglades
Key West
Miami
Havana
YUCATAN
Mérida
Valladolid
Yucatan Channel
Cozumel
Gulf of Campeche
Veracruz
Campeche
Oaxaca
Villahermosa
Chiapas
Tampico
Matamoros
BELIZE
GUATEMALA
CUBA

CANADA
MANITOBA
SASKATCHEWAN
ONTARIO
QUÉBEC
Winnipeg
NORTH AMERICA
MONTANA
Bismarck
NORTH DAKOTA
St Paul
MINNESOTA
Lake Superior
Lake Huron
Ottawa
Montreal
VT
MAINE
IDAHO
WYOMING
SOUTH DAKOTA
WISCONSIN
MICHIGAN
Lake Michigan
Toronto
Lake Ontario
NEW HAMPSHIRE
MASSACHUSETTS
IOWA
Detroit
NEW YORK
RI
CONNECTICUT
Salt Lake City
Omaha
Chicago
Lake Erie
PENNSYLVANIA
New York
NEW JERSEY
UTAH
Denver
NEBRASKA
ILLINOIS
INDIANA
OHIO
MARYLAND
DELAWARE
COLORADO
WEST VIRGINIA
Washington D.C.
KANSAS
MISSOURI
KENTUCKY
VIRGINIA
Las Vegas
UNITED STATES
ARIZONA
OKLAHOMA
TENNESSEE
NORTH CAROLINA
Phoenix
NEW MEXICO
ARKANSAS
Atlanta
SOUTH CAROLINA
Tucson
Hamilton
Fort Worth
ALABAMA
GEORGIA
Bermuda
(UK)
El Paso
Dallas
MISSISSIPPI
TEXAS
LOUISIANA
Mobile
Jacksonville
Houston
New Orleans
Gulf of California
Chihuahua
Rio Grande
FLORIDA
Monterrey
GULF OF
MEXICO
Miami
BAHAMAS
Mazatlán
Turks & Caicos Islands
(UK)
San Luis Potosi
Havana
Greater Antilles
MEXICO
CUBA
PUERTO RICO
Mérida
Cayman Islands
(UK)
HAITI
Virgin Islands
Mexico City
Veracruz
JAMAICA
DOMINICAN
REPUBLIC
BELIZE
Juchitan
HONDURAS
CARIBBEAN SEA
Aruba (NETH)
GUATEMALA
Tegucigalpa
Panama
Canal
EL SALVADOR
NICARAGUA
VENEZUELA
Caracas

Awesome! Now that you've read all about the study of Geography, you may want to read about time and climate zones in the Baby Professor book World Geography–Time & Climates Zones–Latitude, Longitude, Tropics, Meridian and More | Geography for Kids.

Visit

www.BabyProfessorBooks.com

to download Free Baby Professor eBooks
and view our catalog of new and exciting
Children's Books